Singapore MATH

MENTAL MATH

Strategies and Process Skills to Develop Mental Calculation

Grade 4
(Level 3)

Frank Schaffer

An imprint of Carson-Dellosa Publishing LLC

Greensboro, North Carolina

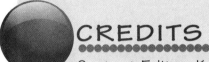

CREDITS

Content Editor: Karen Cermak-Serfass
Copy Editor: Barrie Hoople
Layout Design: Van Harris

This book has been correlated to state, common core state, national, and Canadian provincial standards. Visit www.carsondellosa.com to search for and view its correlations to your standards.

Welcome to Singapore Math! The national math curriculum used in Singapore has been recognized worldwide for its excellence in producing students highly skilled in mathematics. The country's students have ranked at the top in achievement in the world on the Trends in International Mathematics and Science Study (TIMSS) in 1993, 1995, 2003, and 2008. The study also shows that students in Singapore are typically one grade level ahead of students in the United States. Because of these trends, Singapore Math has gained interest and popularity.

Mathematics in the Singapore primary (elementary) curriculum covers fewer topics but in greater depth. Key math concepts are introduced and built upon to reinforce various mathematical ideas and thinking. Singapore Math curriculum aims to help students develop the necessary math process skills for everyday life and to provide students with the opportunity to master math concepts.

Mental Math Level 3, for grade 4, provides a comprehensive guide for mastering mental calculation. Each strategy in this book helps students perform mental calculation and obtain accurate answers in the shortest possible amount of time.

This book consists of 52 practice and review pages. Each practice page demonstrates a strategy with an example and includes 10 problems for students to solve. Students can then test their understanding by working on the review pages that are located after the practice pages.

To help students build and strengthen their mental calculation skills, this book provides strategies that will benefit students as they learn tips to solve math problems quickly and effectively. After acquiring such invaluable skills, students can apply them to their future, real-life experiences with math, such as in shopping and banking. *Mental Math Level 3* is an indispensable resource for all students who wish to master mental strategies and excel in them.

TABLE OF CONTENTS

TABLE OF CONTENTS

STRATEGIES OVERVIEW

The following overview provides examples of the various math problem types and skill sets taught in Singapore Math.

1 Adding Using Place Values

1,286 + 513
= 1,000 + 200 + 80 + 6 + 500 + 10 + 3
      ❏ Expand the numbers by their place values.
      ❏ Add the similar values.
= 1,000 + (200 + 500) + (80 + 10) + (6 + 3)
= 1,000 + 700 + 90 + 9
= **1,799**

2 Adding Doubles

2,516 + 6 = 2,510 + 6 + 6
      ❏ Identify the doubles and add them.
      = 2,510 + 12
      ❏ Add the numbers to find the answer.
      = **2,522**

3 Adding Near Doubles

4,613 + 14 = (4,613 + 1) + 14 − 1
      ❏ Add 1 to 4,613 to create a double.
      = (4,614 + 14) − 1
      ❏ Add the doubles.
      = 4,628 − 1
      ❏ Subtract 1 to find the answer.
      = **4,627**

4 Addition: Rounding Numbers (Part 1)

2,734 + 999 = (2,734 + 1,000) − 1
      ❏ Round 999 up to the nearest thousand. Add 1,000 to the number.
      = 3,734 − 1
      ❏ Subtract 1 to find the answer.
      = **3,733**

5 Addition: Rounding Numbers (Part 2)

4,462 + 998 = (4,462 + 1,000) − 2
      ❏ Round 998 up to the nearest thousand. Add 1,000 to the number.
      = 5,462 − 2
      ❏ Subtract 2 to find the answer.
      = **5,460**

7 Addition: Rounding Numbers (Part 3)

4,229 + 179

179 + 21 = 200
      ❏ Round 179 up to the nearest hundred by adding 21.
4,229 + 179 = (4,229 − 21) + (179 + 21)
      ❏ Since 21 was added to make 200, subtract 21 from 4,229.
      = 4,208 + 200
      ❏ Add the numbers to find the answer.
      = **4,408**

8 Adding Thousands

3,000 + 5,000 = 3 thousands + 5 thousands
      ❏ Read the numbers by their place values and add them.
      = 8 thousands
      = **8,000**

9 Adding a String of Numbers

102 + 103 + 107 + 109 + 111 + 108
= (102 + 108) + (103 + 107) + (109 + 111)
      ❏ Arrange the numbers so that they can be added to the nearest ten. Then, add to find the answer.
= 210 + 210 + 220
= **640**

10 Subtracting Using Place Values

2,573 − 45 = (2,000 + 500 + 70 + 3) − (40 + 5)
      ❏ Expand the numbers.
      = 2,000 + 500 + (60 + 13) − (40 + 5)
      ❏ Regroup one ten.
      = (2,000 + 500) + (60 − 40) + (13 − 5)
      ❏ Subtract. Then, add to find the answer.
      = **2,528**

11 Subtracting Doubles

6,122 − 11 = 6,100 + (22 − 11)
      ❏ Identify the doubles and subtract them.
      = 6,100 + 11
      ❏ Add the numbers to find the answer.
      = **6,111**

13 Subtracting Near Doubles

6,817 − 18 = (6,817 + 1) − 18 − 1
      ❏ Add 1 to the minuend to create a double. This will make 6,818.
      = (6,818 − 18) − 1
      ❏ Subtract the double.
      = 6,800 − 1
      ❏ Subtract 1 to find the answer.
      = **6,799**

14 Subtraction: Rounding Numbers (Part 1)

6,125 − 999 = (6,125 − 1,000) + 1
      ❏ Round 999 up to the nearest thousand. Subtract 1,000 from the minuend.
      = 5,125 + 1
      ❏ Add 1 to find the answer.
      = **5,126**

15 Subtraction: Rounding Numbers (Part 2)

7,232 − 998 = (7,232 − 1,000) + 2
      ❏ Round 998 up to the nearest thousand. Subtract 1,000 from the minuend.
      = 6,232 + 2
      ❏ Add 2 to find the answer.
      = **6,234**

16 Subtraction: Rounding Numbers (Part 3)

3,815 − 286 = (3,815 + 14) − (286 + 14)
      ❏ Round 286 up to the nearest hundred by adding 14 and add 14 to 3,815.
      = 3,829 − 300
      ❏ Subtract the numbers to find the answer.
      = **3,529**

17 Subtracting Thousands

8,000 − 7,000 = 8 thousands − 7 thousands
      ❏ Read the numbers by their place values and subtract them.
      = 1 thousand
      = **1,000**

19 Multiplying Numbers by 6

5 × 6 = 5 × 2 × 3
      ❏ Break up the second factor for easy multiplication with the first factor.
      = (5 × 2) × 3
      = 10 × 3
      ❏ Multiply the numbers to find the answer.
      = **30**

20 Multiplying Numbers by 7

8 × 7 = (5 × 7) + (3 × 7)
      ❏ Break up the first factor into numbers that you are confident in multiplying.
      = 35 + 21
      ❏ Add the numbers to find the answer.
      = **56**

21 Multiplying Numbers by 8

5 × 8 = (3 × 8) + (2 × 8)
      ❏ Break up the first factor into numbers that you are confident in multiplying.
      = 24 + 16
      ❏ Add the numbers to find the answer.
      = **40**

22 Multiplying Numbers by 9

This is a simple method to help you with the multiplication table of 9.

1 × 9 = 9   ❏ Bend the little finger of your left hand, and count 9 fingers. Therefore, the answer is 9.

2 × 9 = 18   ❏ Bend the ring finger of your left hand, and you will notice that 1 finger is on the left and 8 fingers are on the right. Therefore, the answer is 18.

3 × 9 = 27   ❏ Bend the middle finger of your left hand, and you will notice that 2 fingers are on the left and 7 fingers are on the right. Therefore, the answer is 27.

4 × 9 = 36   ❏ Bend the index finger of your left hand, and you will notice that 3 fingers are on the left and 6 fingers are on the right. Therefore, the answer is 36.

5 × 9 = 45   ❏ Bend the thumb of your left hand, and you will notice that 4 fingers are on the left and 5 fingers are on the right. Therefore, the answer is 45.

6 × 9 = 54   ❏ Bend the thumb of your right hand, and you will notice that 5 fingers are on the left and 4 fingers are on the right. Therefore, the answer is 54.

7 × 9 = 63   ❏ Bend the index finger of your right hand, and you will notice that 6 fingers are on the left and 3 fingers are on the right. Therefore, the answer is 63.

8 × 9 = 72   ❏ Bend the middle finger of your right hand, and you will notice that 7 fingers are on the left and 2 fingers are on the right. Therefore, the answer is 72.

9 × 9 = 81   ❏ Bend the ring finger of your right hand, and you will notice that 8 fingers are on the left and 1 finger is on the right. Therefore, the answer is 81.

10 × 9 = 90   ❏ Bend the little finger of your right hand, and you will notice that 9 fingers are on the left. Therefore, the answer is 90.

23 Multiplying Numbers by 11

6 × 11 = **66**
❑ Any one-digit number multiplied by 11 will have a two-digit answer that is identical to the single digit.

25 Multiplying Numbers by 12

8 × 12 = (8 × 10) + (8 × 2)
❑ Break up the factor 12 into 10 and 2 for easy multiplication.

= 80 + 16
❑ Add the numbers to find the answer.
= **96**

26 Multiplication: Rounding Numbers (Part 1)

49 × 6

49 ≈ 50
❑ Round the two-digit factor up to the nearest ten.

49 × 6 = (50 – 1) × 6
❑ Subtract 1 since 1 was added to 49 to make 50.

= (50 × 6) – (1 × 6)
❑ Multiply each number by the one-digit factor.

= 300 – 6
❑ Subtract the numbers to find the answer.
= **294**

27 Multiplication: Rounding Numbers (Part 2)

199 × 8

199 ≈ 200
❑ Round the three-digit factor up to the nearest hundred.

199 × 8 = (200 – 1) × 8
❑ Subtract 1 since 1 was added to 199 to make 200.

= (200 × 8) – (1 × 8)
❑ Multiply each number by the one-digit factor.

= 1,600 – 8
❑ Subtract the numbers to find the answer.
= **1,592**

28 Multiplication: Breaking Up Numbers (Part 1)

34 × 7 = (30 × 7) + (4 × 7)
❑ Break up the factor 34 into 30 and 4. Multiply each part by the one-digit factor.

= 210 + 28
❑ Add the numbers to find the answer.
= **238**

29 Multiplication: Breaking Up Numbers (Part 2)

128 × 9 = (100 × 9) + (20 × 9) + (8 × 9)
❑ Break up the factor 128 into 100, 20, and 8. Multiply each number by the one-digit factor.

= 900 + 180 + 72
❑ Add the numbers to find the answer.
= **1,152**

31 Divisibility Rule of 2

A number can be divided by 2 if the last digit of the number is even.

Can 238 be divided by 2?

❑ Look at the last digit. The last digit, 8, is an even number.

Therefore, 238 can be divided by 2.

32 Divisibility Rule of 3

A number can be divided by 3 if the sum of all of the digits is divisible by 3.

Can 147 be divided by 3?

1 + 4 + 7 = 12
❑ Add all of the digits.

12 ÷ 3 = 4
❑ Divide the sum by 3. The sum, 12, is divisible by 3.

Therefore, 147 can be divided by 3.

33 Divisibility Rule of 4

A number can be divided by 4 if the last two digits of the number are divisible by 4.

Can 128 be divided by 4?

28 ÷ 4 = 7
❑ Divide the last two digits by 4. The last two digits, 28, are divisible by 4.

Therefore, 128 can be divided by 4.

34 Divisibility Rule of 5

A number can be divided by 5 if the last digit of the number is a 0 or a 5.

Can 550 be divided by 5?

❑ Look at the last digit. The last digit is 0.

Therefore, 550 can be divided by 5.

35 Divisibility Rule of 6

A number can be divided by 6 if it can be divided by both 2 and 3.

Can 198 be divided by 6?

8
❑ Look at the last digit. The last digit, 8, is an even number.

1 + 9 + 8 = 18
❑ Add all of the digits.

18 ÷ 3 = 6
❑ Divide the sum by 3. The sum, 18, is divisible by 3.

Therefore, 198 can be divided by 6.

37 Divisibility Rule of 7

To determine if a number can be divided by 7, double the last digit in the number. Then, subtract the answer from the rest of the number. If the difference can be divided by 7, the number is divisible by 7.

Can 385 be divided by 7?

5 × 2 = 10
❑ Multiply the last digit in the number by 2.

38 – 10 = 28
❑ Subtract the product from the remaining digits.

28 ÷ 7 = 4
❑ Divide the difference by 7. The difference, 28, is divisible by 7.

Therefore, 385 can be divided by 7.

38 Divisibility Rule of 9

A number can be divided by 9 if the sum of all of the digits is divisible by 9.

Can 297 be divided by 9?

2 + 9 + 7 = 18
❑ Add all of the digits.

18 ÷ 9 = 2
❑ Divide the sum by 9. The sum, 18, is divisible by 9.

Therefore, 297 can be divided by 9.

39 Divisibility Rule of 10

A number can be divided by 10 if the last digit of the number is 0.

Can 120 be divided by 10?

❑ Look at the last digit. The last digit is 0.

Therefore, 120 can be divided by 10.

40 Divisibility Rule of 11

To determine if a number can be divided by 11, add the alternating digits and subtract the remaining digits from the sum. If the answer is 0 or a number that can be divided by 11, then it is divisible by 11.

Can 231 be divided by 11?

2 + 1 = 3
❑ Add the digits in the hundreds and ones places.

3 – 3 = 0
❑ Subtract the sum from the digit in the tens place. The answer is 0.

Therefore, 231 can be divided by 11.

41 Divisibility Rule of 12

A number can be divided by 12 if it can be divided by both 3 and 4.

Can 216 be divided by 12?

2 + 1 + 6 = 9
❑ Add all of the digits.

9 ÷ 3 = 3
❑ Divide the sum by 3. The sum, 9, is divisible by 3.

16 ÷ 4 = 4
❑ Divide the last two digits by 4. The last two digits, 16, are divisible by 4.

Therefore, 216 can be divided by 12.

43 Division: Breaking Up Numbers (Part 1)

175 ÷ 7 = (140 ÷ 7) + (35 ÷ 7)
❑ Break up the dividend 175 into smaller numbers. Divide each part by the divisor.

= 20 + 5
❑ Add the numbers to find the answer.
= **25**

44 Division: Breaking Up Numbers (Part 2)

432 ÷ 9 = (432 ÷ 3) ÷ 3
❑ Break up the divisor 9 into smaller numbers.

= 144 ÷ 3
❑ Divide again to find the answer.
= **48**

STRATEGY

Adding Using Place Values

Strategy

$1,286 + 513 = 1,000 + 200 + 80 + 6 + 500 + 10 + 3$

$= 1,000 + (200 + 500) + (80 + 10) + (6 + 3)$

$= 1,000 + 700 + 90 + 9$

$= \mathbf{1,799}$

❏ Expand the numbers by their place values.

❏ Add the similar values.

Solve each problem mentally.

1. $2,064 + 325 =$

2. $4,253 + 242 =$

3. $6,261 + 436 =$

4. $8,234 + 641 =$

5. $4,040 + 937 =$

6. $5,555 + 243 =$

7. $9,264 + 111 =$

8. $7,042 + 626 =$

9. $1,733 + 245 =$

10. $4,271 + 707 =$

Adding Doubles

Strategy

$2{,}516 + 6 = 2{,}510 + 6 + 6$ ❑ Identify the doubles and add them.
$= 2{,}510 + 12$ ❑ Add the numbers to find the answer.
$= \mathbf{2{,}522}$

Solve each problem mentally.

1. $9{,}708 + 8 \ =$

2. $6{,}012 + 12 =$

3. $3{,}259 + 9 \ =$

4. $1{,}724 + 24 =$

5. $8{,}911 + 11 =$

6. $4{,}805 + 5 \ =$

7. $7{,}725 + 25 =$

8. $5{,}013 + 13 =$

9. $9{,}923 + 23 =$

10. $1{,}817 + 7 \ =$

Adding Near Doubles

Strategy

$4,613 + 14 = (4,613 + 1) + 14 - 1$ ❑ Add 1 to 4,613 to create a double. This will make 4,614.

$= (4,614 + 14) - 1$ ❑ Add the doubles.

$= 4,628 - 1$ ❑ Subtract 1 to find the answer.

$= \mathbf{4,627}$

Solve each problem mentally.

1. $8,211 + 12 =$

2. $1,427 + 8 \ \ =$

3. $6,214 + 15 =$

4. $5,235 + 6 \ \ =$

5. $2,008 + 9 \ \ =$

6. $3,723 + 24 =$

7. $7,620 + 21 =$

8. $4,315 + 16 =$

9. $1,906 + 7 \ \ =$

10. $9,913 + 14 =$

Addition: Rounding Numbers (Part 1)

Strategy

$2,734 + 999 = (2,734 + 1,000) - 1$ ❑ Round 999 up to the nearest thousand.
Add 1,000 to the number.

$= 3,734 - 1$ ❑ Subtract 1 to find the answer.
$= \mathbf{3,733}$

Helpful Hint: As you work, look for a pattern in your answers.

Solve each problem mentally.

1. $2,845 + 999 =$

2. $7,331 + 999 =$

3. $3,258 + 999 =$

4. $4,853 + 999 =$

5. $1,472 + 999 =$

6. $8,221 + 999 =$

7. $5,347 + 999 =$

8. $6,210 + 999 =$

9. $1,111 + 999 =$

10. $3,692 + 999 =$

STRATEGY

Addition: Rounding Numbers (Part 2)

Strategy

$4,462 + 998 = (4,462 + 1,000) - 2$ ❑ Round 998 up to the nearest thousand. Add 1,000 to the number.

$= 5,462 - 2$ ❑ Subtract 2 to find the answer.

$= \textbf{5,460}$

Note: This strategy can be used to add 996 and 997. Subtract 4 or 3 after adding 1,000 to the number to find the answer.

Solve each problem mentally.

1. $5,215 + 998 =$

2. $3,924 + 997 =$

3. $7,243 + 997 =$

4. $1,663 + 998 =$

5. $2,587 + 997 =$

6. $4,298 + 997 =$

7. $3,046 + 996 =$

8. $6,517 + 998 =$

9. $8,125 + 997 =$

10. $4,296 + 996 =$

GENERAL REVIEW 1

Solve each problem mentally.

1. 5,037 + 802 =

2. 2,311 + 12 =

3. 6,275 + 999 =

4. 2,132 + 457 =

5. 3,284 + 996 =

6. 9,247 + 7 =

7. 5,307 + 8 =

8. 1,792 + 996 =

9. 7,122 + 999 =

10. 7,122 + 22 =

Addition: Rounding Numbers (Part 3)

Strategy

$4,229 + 179$

$179 + 21 = 200$ ❑ Round 179 up to the nearest hundred by adding 21.

$4,229 + 179 = (4,229 - 21) + (179 + 21)$ ❑ Since 21 was added to make 200, subtract 21 from 4,229.

$= 4,208 + 200$ ❑ Add the numbers to find the answer.

$= \mathbf{4,408}$

Solve each problem mentally.

1. $4,269 + 248 =$

2. $6,234 + 389 =$

3. $1,138 + 674 =$

4. $2,763 + 948 =$

5. $3,336 + 165 =$

6. $8,250 + 462 =$

7. $5,452 + 266 =$

8. $7,844 + 396 =$

9. $8,761 + 779 =$

10. $4,776 + 278 =$

Adding Thousands

Strategy

3,000 + 5,000 = 3 thousands + 5 thousands   ❑ Read the numbers by their place values and add them.

= 8 thousands

= **8,000**

Solve each problem mentally.

1.   2,000 + 5,000 =

2.   5,000 + 4,000 =

3.   1,000 + 6,000 =

4.   3,000 + 3,000 =

5.   7,000 + 2,000 =

6.   2,000 + 3,000 =

7.   8,000 + 1,000 =

8.   5,000 + 2,000 =

9.   4,000 + 4,000 =

10.   7,000 + 1,000 =

STRATEGY

Adding a String of Numbers

Strategy

102 + 103 + 107 + 109 + 111 + 108
= (102 + 108) + (103 + 107) + (109 + 111)   ☐ Arrange the numbers so that they can be added to the nearest ten. Then, add each pair of numbers.

= 210 + 210 + 220
= **640**   ☐ Add the numbers to find the answer.

Solve each problem mentally.

1. 209 + 102 + 201 + 108 =

2. 216 + 127 + 103 + 304 =

3. 112 + 8 + 109 + 5 + 101 + 335 =

4. 517 + 104 + 3 + 206 + 212 + 108 =

5. 214 + 301 + 212 + 109 + 116 + 18 =

6. 121 + 404 + 155 + 209 + 106 + 305 =

7. 443 + 218 + 302 + 227 + 207 + 103 =

8. 312 + 208 + 173 + 225 + 207 + 105 =

9. 229 + 526 + 124 + 101 + 406 + 304 =

10. 813 + 214 + 107 + 386 + 306 + 104 =

STRATEGY

Subtracting Using Place Values

Strategy

$2,573 - 45$
$= (2,000 + 500 + 70 + 3) - (40 + 5)$

❑ Expand the numbers by their place values.

$= 2,000 + 500 + (60 + 13) - (40 + 5)$

❑ Regroup one ten to the ones place.

$= 2,000 + 500 + (60 - 40) + (13 - 5)$

❑ Arrange the numbers to subtract the tens and the ones values.

$= 2,500 + 20 + 8$

❑ Add the numbers to find the answer.

$= \textbf{2,528}$

Solve each problem mentally.

1. $9,273 - 47 =$

2. $1,765 - 39 =$

3. $5,271 - 33 =$

4. $8,286 - 68 =$

5. $4,244 - 27 =$

6. $6,782 - 76 =$

7. $7,453 - 18 =$

8. $3,997 - 89 =$

9. $2,891 - 58 =$

10. $6,074 - 66 =$

STRATEGY

Subtracting Doubles

Strategy

$6,122 - 11 = 6,100 + (22 - 11)$ ❏ Identify the doubles and subtract them.
$= 6,100 + 11$ ❏ Add the numbers to find the answer.
$= \mathbf{6,111}$

Helpful Hint: As you work, look for a pattern in your answers.

Solve each problem mentally.

1. $5,324 - 12 =$

2. $8,430 - 15 =$

3. $6,336 - 18 =$

4. $7,060 - 30 =$

5. $1,288 - 44 =$

6. $4,764 - 32 =$

7. $2,856 - 28 =$

8. $9,388 - 44 =$

9. $7,238 - 19 =$

10. $6,974 - 37 =$

GENERAL REVIEW 2

Solve each problem mentally.

1. 2,000 + 6,000 =

2. 5,349 + 268 =

3. 208 + 136 + 522 + 304 =

4. 6,476 – 39 =

5. 1,983 – 58 =

6. 7,129 + 482 =

7. 7,866 – 33 =

8. 4,000 + 3,000 =

9. 2,126 – 13 =

10. 519 + 116 + 124 + 321 =

STRATEGY

Subtracting Near Doubles

Strategy

$6,817 - 18 = (6,817 + 1) - 18 - 1$ ❑ Add 1 to the minuend to create a double. This will make 6,818.

$= (6,818 - 18) - 1$ ❑ Subtract the double.

$= 6,800 - 1$ ❑ Subtract 1 to find the answer.

$= \mathbf{6,799}$

Solve each problem mentally.

1. $2,449 - 50 =$

2. $5,612 - 13 =$

3. $9,327 - 28 =$

4. $3,642 - 43 =$

5. $4,916 - 17 =$

6. $6,338 - 39 =$

7. $8,415 - 16 =$

8. $1,955 - 56 =$

9. $7,322 - 23 =$

10. $9,840 - 41 =$

STRATEGY

Subtraction: Rounding Numbers (Part 1)

Strategy

$6{,}125 - 999 = (6{,}125 - 1{,}000) + 1$ ❑ Round 999 up to the nearest thousand. Subtract 1,000 from the minuend.

$\qquad = 5{,}125 + 1$ ❑ Add 1 to find the answer.

$\qquad = \mathbf{5{,}126}$

Helpful Hint: As you work, look for a pattern in your answers.

Solve each problem mentally.

1. $3{,}027 - 999 =$

2. $7{,}183 - 999 =$

3. $1{,}628 - 999 =$

4. $9{,}135 - 999 =$

5. $5{,}168 - 999 =$

6. $2{,}497 - 999 =$

7. $6{,}320 - 999 =$

8. $4{,}563 - 999 =$

9. $8{,}028 - 999 =$

10. $5{,}634 - 999 =$

STRATEGY

Subtraction: Rounding Numbers (Part 2)

Strategy

7,232 – 998 = (7,232 – 1,000) + 2 ❑ Round 998 up to the nearest thousand.
Subtract 1,000 from the minuend.

= 6,232 + 2 ❑ Add 2 to find the answer.

= **6,234**

Note: This strategy can be used to subtract 996 or 997. Add 4 or 3
after subtracting 1,000 from the minuend to find the answer.

Solve each problem mentally.

1. 7,534 – 998 =

2. 9,120 – 996 =

3. 3,475 – 996 =

4. 5,791 – 998 =

5. 8,163 – 996 =

6. 1,278 – 997 =

7. 6,160 – 998 =

8. 4,352 – 998 =

9. 2,438 – 996 =

10. 5,373 – 997 =

STRATEGY

Subtraction: Rounding Numbers (Part 3)

Strategy

$3,815 - 286 = (3,815 + 14) - (286 + 14)$ ❑ Round 286 up to the nearest hundred by adding 14 and add 14 to 3,815.

$= 3,829 - 300$ ❑ Subtract the numbers to find the answer.

$= \textbf{3,529}$

Solve each problem mentally.

1. $1,826 - 387 =$

2. $5,822 - 163 =$

3. $9,034 - 845 =$

4. $2,573 - 686 =$

5. $7,511 - 271 =$

6. $3,567 - 588 =$

7. $8,161 - 466 =$

8. $6,310 - 781 =$

9. $4,827 - 569 =$

10. $6,852 - 873 =$

STRATEGY

Subtracting Thousands

Strategy

8,000 – 7,000 = 8 thousands – 7 thousands ❑ Read the numbers by their place values and subtract them.

= 1 thousand
= **1,000**

Solve each problem mentally.

1. 6,000 – 3,000 =

2. 9,000 – 2,000 =

3. 3,000 – 2,000 =

4. 5,000 – 1,000 =

5. 8,000 – 2,000 =

6. 7,000 – 5,000 =

7. 4,000 – 2,000 =

8. 9,000 – 4,000 =

9. 6,000 – 2,000 =

10. 5,000 – 3,000 =

GENERAL REVIEW 3

Solve each problem mentally.

1. 4,323 − 24 =

2. 6,000 − 5,000 =

3. 7,534 − 188 =

4. 8,032 − 999 =

5. 5,634 − 996 =

6. 1,948 − 49 =

7. 4,328 − 999 =

8. 9,000 − 6,000 =

9. 3,609 − 345 =

10. 6,714 − 998 =

STRATEGY

Multiplying Numbers by 6

Strategy

$5 \times 6 = 5 \times 2 \times 3$

$\quad = (5 \times 2) \times 3$
$\quad = 10 \times 3$
$\quad = \mathbf{30}$

❑ Break up the second factor for easy multiplication with the first factor.

❑ Multiply the numbers to find the answer.

Solve each problem mentally.

1. $10 \times 6 =$

2. $6 \times 6 =$

3. $9 \times 6 =$

4. $4 \times 6 =$

5. $11 \times 6 =$

6. $8 \times 6 =$

7. $2 \times 6 =$

8. $7 \times 6 =$

9. $12 \times 6 =$

10. $3 \times 6 =$

STRATEGY

Multiplying Numbers by 7

Strategy

$8 × 7 = (5 × 7) + (3 × 7)$ ❑ Break up the first factor into numbers that you are confident in multiplying. In this case, it can be 5 and 3 because you have learned these two multiplication tables before.

$= 35 + 21$ ❑ Add the numbers to find the answer.

$= \mathbf{56}$

Solve each problem mentally.

1. $4 × 7 =$
2. $9 × 7 =$
3. $3 × 7 =$
4. $12 × 7 =$
5. $7 × 7 =$
6. $6 × 7 =$
7. $5 × 7 =$
8. $11 × 7 =$
9. $2 × 7 =$
10. $10 × 7 =$

STRATEGY

Multiplying Numbers by 8

Strategy

$5 \times 8 = (3 \times 8) + (2 \times 8)$

❑ Break up the first factor into numbers that you are confident in multiplying. In this case, it can be 3 and 2 because you have learned these two multiplication tables before.

$= 24 + 16$

$= \textbf{40}$

❑ Add the numbers to find the answer.

Solve each problem mentally.

1. $3 \times 8 =$

2. $7 \times 8 =$

3. $11 \times 8 =$

4. $6 \times 8 =$

5. $2 \times 8 =$

6. $8 \times 8 =$

7. $10 \times 8 =$

8. $4 \times 8 =$

9. $9 \times 8 =$

10. $12 \times 8 =$

STRATEGY

Multiplying Numbers by 9

Strategy

This is a simple method to help you with the multiplication table of 9. Bend the finger for each number that you are multiplying by 9 and count the digits on each side of the bent finger.

$1 \times 9 = 9$ ❑ Bend the little finger of your left hand, and count 9 fingers. Therefore, the answer is 9.

$2 \times 9 = 18$ ❑ Bend the ring finger of your left hand, and you will notice that 1 finger is on the left and 8 fingers are on the right. Therefore, the answer is 18.

$3 \times 9 = 27$ ❑ Bend the middle finger of your left hand, and you will notice that 2 fingers are on the left and 7 fingers are on the right. Therefore, the answer is 27.

$4 \times 9 = 36$ ❑ Bend the index finger of your left hand, and you will notice that 3 fingers are on the left and 6 fingers are on the right. Therefore, the answer is 36.

$5 \times 9 = 45$ ❑ Bend the thumb of your left hand, and you will notice that 4 fingers are on the left and 5 fingers are on the right. Therefore, the answer is 45.

$6 \times 9 = 54$ ❑ Bend the thumb of your right hand, and you will notice that 5 fingers are on the left and 4 fingers are on the right. Therefore, the answer is 54.

$7 \times 9 = 63$ ❑ Bend the index finger of your right hand, and you will notice that 6 fingers are on the left and 3 fingers are on the right. Therefore, the answer is 63.

$8 \times 9 = 72$ ❑ Bend the middle finger of your right hand, and you will notice that 7 fingers are on the left and 2 fingers are on the right. Therefore, the answer is 72.

$9 \times 9 = 81$ ❑ Bend the ring finger of your right hand, and you will notice that 8 fingers are on the left and 1 finger is on the right. Therefore, the answer is 81.

$10 \times 9 = 90$ ❑ Bend the little finger of your right hand, and you will notice that 9 fingers are on the left. Therefore, the answer is 90.

Solve each problem mentally.

1. $10 \times 9 =$

2. $5 \times 9 =$

3. $3 \times 9 =$

4. $1 \times 9 =$

5. $7 \times 9 =$

6. $4 \times 9 =$

7. $2 \times 9 =$

8. $6 \times 9 =$

9. $8 \times 9 =$

10. $9 \times 9 =$

STRATEGY

Multiplying Numbers by 11

Strategy

$6 \times 11 = $ **66** ❑ Any one-digit number multiplied by 11 will have a two-digit answer that is identical to the single digit.

Solve each problem mentally.

1. $9 \times 11 = $

2. $12 \times 11 = $

3. $1 \times 11 = $

4. $5 \times 11 = $

5. $8 \times 11 = $

6. $11 \times 11 = $

7. $4 \times 11 = $

8. $3 \times 11 = $

9. $7 \times 11 = $

10. $2 \times 11 = $

GENERAL REVIEW 4

Solve each problem mentally.

1. 5 × 9 =

2. 7 × 6 =

3. 9 × 8 =

4. 4 × 7 =

5. 12 × 11 =

6. 4 × 8 =

7. 7 × 9 =

8. 5 × 6 =

9. 12 × 7 =

10. 6 × 11 =

Multiplying Numbers by 12

Strategy

$8 × 12 = (8 × 10) + (8 × 2)$

$= 80 + 16$

$= \mathbf{96}$

❑ Break up the factor 12 into 10 and 2 for easy multiplication.

❑ Add the numbers to find the answer.

Solve each problem mentally.

1. $5 × 12 =$

2. $10 × 12 =$

3. $2 × 12 =$

4. $7 × 12 =$

5. $9 × 12 =$

6. $12 × 12 =$

7. $3 × 12 =$

8. $6 × 12 =$

9. $4 × 12 =$

10. $11 × 12 =$

Multiplication: Rounding Numbers (Part 1)

Strategy

49×6

$49 \approx 50$ ❑ Round the two-digit factor up to the nearest ten.

$49 \times 6 = (50 - 1) \times 6$ ❑ Subtract 1 since 1 was added to 49 to make 50.

$ = (50 \times 6) - (1 \times 6)$ ❑ Multiply each number by the one-digit factor.

$ = 300 - 6$ ❑ Subtract the numbers to find the answer.

$ = \mathbf{294}$

Solve each problem mentally.

1. $88 \times 7 =$

2. $99 \times 5 =$

3. $37 \times 9 =$

4. $45 \times 2 =$

5. $87 \times 8 =$

6. $79 \times 7 =$

7. $26 \times 6 =$

8. $58 \times 4 =$

9. $67 \times 3 =$

10. $19 \times 8 =$

Multiplication: Rounding Numbers (Part 2)

Strategy

199×8

$199 \approx 200$ ❑ Round the three-digit factor up to the nearest hundred.

$199 \times 8 = (200 - 1) \times 8$ ❑ Subtract 1 since 1 was added to 199 to make 200.

$\quad = (200 \times 8) - (1 \times 8)$ ❑ Multiply each number by the one-digit factor.

$\quad = 1,600 - 8$ ❑ Subtract the numbers to find the answer.

$\quad = \mathbf{1,592}$

Solve each problem mentally.

1. $299 \times 4 \ =$

2. $499 \times 6 \ =$

3. $699 \times 8 \ =$

4. $399 \times 5 \ =$

5. $199 \times 7 \ =$

6. $399 \times 9 \ =$

7. $799 \times 4 \ =$

8. $899 \times 3 \ =$

9. $999 \times 2 \ =$

10. $599 \times 9 \ =$

STRATEGY

Multiplication: Breaking Up Numbers (Part 1)

Strategy

$34 × 7 = (30 × 7) + (4 × 7)$

$= 210 + 28$
$= \mathbf{238}$

❑ Break up the factor 34 into 30 and 4. Multiply each part by the one-digit factor.
❑ Add the numbers to find the answer.

Solve each problem mentally.

1. $86 × 8 =$

2. $47 × 3 =$

3. $26 × 9 =$

4. $53 × 5 =$

5. $74 × 6 =$

6. $64 × 2 =$

7. $95 × 7 =$

8. $43 × 8 =$

9. $96 × 4 =$

10. $56 × 9 =$

Multiplication: Breaking Up Numbers (Part 2)

Strategy

$128 \times 9 = (100 \times 9) + (20 \times 9) + (8 \times 9)$

❑ Break up the factor 128 into 100, 20, and 8. Multiply each number by the one-digit factor.

$= 900 + 180 + 72$

❑ Add the numbers to find the answer.

$= 1,152$

Solve each problem mentally.

1. $462 \times 7 =$

2. $907 \times 4 =$

3. $142 \times 3 =$

4. $273 \times 9 =$

5. $531 \times 7 =$

6. $337 \times 8 =$

7. $628 \times 5 =$

8. $389 \times 6 =$

9. $854 \times 7 =$

10. $960 \times 2 =$

GENERAL REVIEW 5

Solve each problem mentally.

1.	89 × 9 =
2.	199 × 3 =
3.	68 × 8 =
4.	162 × 4 =
5.	24 × 9 =
6.	38 × 7 =
7.	93 × 5 =
8.	374 × 6 =
9.	599 × 3 =
10.	7 × 12 =

Divisibility Rule of 2

Strategy

A number can be divided by 2 if the last digit of the number is even.

Can 238 be divided by 2?

❑ Look at the last digit. The last digit, 8, is an even number.

Therefore, 238 can be divided by 2.

Can these numbers be divided by 2? Write *Yes* or *No*.

1. 856

2. 907

3. 125

4. 340

5. 558

6. 734

7. 493

8. 642

9. 284

10. 847

Divisibility Rule of 3

Strategy

A number can be divided by 3 if the sum of all of the digits is divisible by 3. Can 147 be divided by 3?

1 + 4 + 7 = 12   ❏ Add all of the digits.

12 ÷ 3 = 4   ❏ Divide the sum by 3. The sum, 12, is divisible by 3.

Therefore, 147 can be divided by 3.

Can these numbers be divided by 3? Write *Yes* or *No*.

1. 361

2. 165

3. 207

4. 819

5. 625

6. 991

7. 726

8. 543

9. 489

10. 764

Divisibility Rule of 4

Strategy

A number can be divided by 4 if the last two digits of the number are divisible by 4.

Can 128 be divided by 4?

28 ÷ 4 = 7 ❑ Divide the last two digits by 4. The last two digits, 28, are divisible by 4.

Therefore, 128 can be divided by 4.

Can these numbers be divided by 4? Write *Yes* or *No*.

1. 506

2. 912

3. 218

4. 135

5. 848

6. 616

7. 925

8. 736

9. 420

10. 327

Divisibility Rule of 5

Strategy

A number can be divided by 5 if the last digit of the number is a 0 or a 5.

Can 550 be divided by 5?

❑ Look at the last digit. The last digit is 0.

Therefore, 550 can be divided by 5.

Can these numbers be divided by 5? Write Yes or No.

1.	315	
2.	884	
3.	460	
4.	728	
5.	570	
6.	900	
7.	293	
8.	616	
9.	390	
10.	995	

Divisibility Rule of 6

Strategy

A number can be divided by 6 if it can be divided by both 2 and 3.
A number can be divided by 2 if the last digit of the number is even.
A number can be divided by 3 if the sum of all of the digits is divisible by 3.
Can 198 be divided by 6?

8	❑ Look at the last digit. The last digit, 8, is an even number.
1 + 9 + 8 = 18	❑ Add all of the digits.
18 ÷ 3 = 6	❑ Divide the sum by 3. The sum, 18, is divisible by 3.

Therefore, 198 can be divided by 6.

Can these numbers be divided by 6? Write *Yes* or *No*.

1. 534

2. 923

3. 294

4. 716

5. 497

6. 654

7. 588

8. 396

9. 154

10. 804

WEEK **36**

GENERAL REVIEW 6

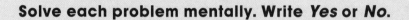

Solve each problem mentally. Write *Yes* or *No*.

1. Can 579 be divided by 3?

2. Can 275 be divided by 2?

3. Can 836 be divided by 6?

4. Can 195 be divided by 4?

5. Can 580 be divided by 5?

6. Can 751 be divided by 2?

7. Can 694 be divided by 4?

8. Can 432 be divided by 6?

9. Can 886 be divided by 3?

10. Can 305 be divided by 5?

Divisibility Rule of 7

Strategy

To determine if a number can be divided by 7, double the last digit in the number. Then, subtract the answer from the rest of the number. If the difference can be divided by 7, the number is divisible by 7.

Can 385 be divided by 7?

$5 \times 2 = 10$	❑ Multiply the last digit in the number by 2.
$38 - 10 = 28$	❑ Subtract the product from the remaining digits.
$28 \div 7 = 4$	❑ Divide the difference by 7. The difference, 28, is divisible by 7.

Therefore, 385 can be divided by 7.

Can these numbers be divided by 7? Write *Yes* or *No*.

1. 441
2. 616
3. 519
4. 219
5. 688
6. 273
7. 339
8. 507
9. 735
10. 955

STRATEGY

Divisibility Rule of 9

Strategy

A number can be divided by 9 if the sum of all of the digits is divisible by 9.
Can 297 be divided by 9?

2 + 9 + 7 = 18   ❏ Add all of the digits.

18 ÷ 9 = 2   ❏ Divide the sum by 9. The sum, 18, is divisible by 9.

Therefore, 297 can be divided by 9.

Can these numbers be divided by 9? Write *Yes* or *No*.

1. 441

2. 149

3. 252

4. 504

5. 816

6. 991

7. 342

8. 798

9. 684

10. 867

STRATEGY

Divisibility Rule of 10

Strategy

A number can be divided by 10 if the last digit of the number is 0.

Can 120 be divided by 10?

❏ Look at the last digit. The last digit is 0.

Therefore, 120 can be divided by 10.

Can these numbers be divided by 10? Write *Yes* or *No*.

1. 335

2. 600

3. 190

4. 404

5. 891

6. 970

7. 595

8. 290

9. 387

10. 740

Divisibility Rule of 11

Strategy

To determine if a number can be divided by 11, add the alternating digits and subtract the remaining digits from the sum. If the answer is 0 or a number that can be divided by 11, then it is divisible by 11.

Can 231 be divided by 11?

2 + 1 = 3	❏ Add the digits in the hundreds and ones places.
3 − 3 = 0	❏ Subtract the sum from the digit in the tens place. The answer is 0.

Therefore, 231 can be divided by 11.

Can these numbers be divided by 11? Write _Yes_ or _No_.

1.	792	
2.	504	
3.	902	
4.	384	
5.	671	
6.	181	
7.	594	
8.	275	
9.	726	
10.	979	

STRATEGY

Divisibility Rule of 12

Strategy

A number can be divided by 12 if it can be divided by both 3 and 4.
A number can be divided by 3 if the sum of all of the digits is divisible by 3.
A number can be divided by 4 if the last two digits of the number are divisible by 4.

Can 216 be divided by 12?

2 + 1 + 6 = 9	❏ Add all of the digits.
9 ÷ 3 = 3	❏ Divide the sum by 3. The sum, 9, is divisible by 3.
16 ÷ 4 = 4	❏ Divide the last two digits by 4. The last two digits, 16, are divisible by 4.

Therefore, 216 can be divided by 12.

Can these numbers be divided by 12? Write *Yes* or *No*.

1. 618

2. 384

3. 192

4. 289

5. 912

6. 764

7. 918

8. 312

9. 456

10. 662

GENERAL REVIEW 7

Solve each problem mentally. Write _Yes_ or _No_.

1. Can 425 be divided by 10?

2. Can 648 be divided by 9?

3. Can 826 be divided by 7?

4. Can 972 be divided by 12?

5. Can 187 be divided by 11?

6. Can 490 be divided by 10?

7. Can 537 be divided by 7?

8. Can 297 be divided by 9?

9. Can 348 be divided by 12?

10. Can 671 be divided by 11?

STRATEGY

Division: Breaking Up Numbers (Part 1)

Strategy

$175 \div 7 = (140 \div 7) + (35 \div 7)$

❑ Break up the dividend 175 into smaller numbers. Divide each part by the divisor.

$= 20 + 5$

❑ Add the numbers to find the answer.

$= \mathbf{25}$

Solve each problem mentally.

1. $184 \div 2 =$

2. $288 \div 8 =$

3. $567 \div 9 =$

4. $147 \div 7 =$

5. $380 \div 5 =$

6. $252 \div 6 =$

7. $189 \div 3 =$

8. $376 \div 4 =$

9. $680 \div 8 =$

10. $495 \div 9 =$

Division: Breaking Up Numbers (Part 2)

Strategy

$432 \div 9 = (432 \div 3) \div 3$ ❑ Break up the divisor 9 into smaller numbers.
$= 144 \div 3$ ❑ Divide again to find the answer.
$= \textbf{48}$

Note: Rely on the Divisibility Rules when deciding how to break up the divisor.

Solve each problem mentally.

1. $520 \div 8 =$

2. $138 \div 6 =$

3. $468 \div 9 =$

4. $328 \div 4 =$

5. $504 \div 8 =$

6. $648 \div 9 =$

7. $282 \div 6 =$

8. $232 \div 8 =$

9. $387 \div 9 =$

10. $444 \div 6 =$

GENERAL REVIEW 8

Solve each problem mentally.

1. 2,321 + 37 =

2. 1,116 – 8 =

3. 9 × 11 =

4. 56 ÷ 8 =

5. 12 × 11 =

6. 4,000 + 5,000 =

7. Can 638 be divided by 4?

8. 336 ÷ 8 =

9. 1,693 – 99 =

10. 105 + 122 + 108 + 255 =

GENERAL REVIEW 9

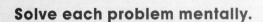

Solve each problem mentally.

1. $54 \div 9 =$

2. $3,824 + 24 =$

3. $1,632 + 33 =$

4. $6 \times 7 =$

5. $128 \div 8 =$

6. Can 486 be divided by 3?

7. $399 \times 4 =$

8. $64 \div 8 =$

9. $3,284 + 997 =$

10. $6,000 + 3,000 =$

GENERAL REVIEW 10

Solve each problem mentally.

1. 8,024 – 999 =

2. 1,243 – 378 =

3. 599 × 8 =

4. 4,963 + 999 =

5. Can 108 be divided by 9?

6. 256 ÷ 8 =

7. 7,014 + 14 =

8. 3,219 – 20 =

9. 12 × 5 =

10. Can 534 be divided by 11?

GENERAL REVIEW 11

Solve each problem mentally.

1. $396 \div 4 =$

2. $42 \times 8 =$

3. $3,749 - 169 =$

4. $6,308 + 997 =$

5. $5,017 + 18 =$

6. $9 \times 9 =$

7. $399 + 204 + 201 + 556 =$

8. $64 \div 8 =$

9. Can 638 be divided by 7?

10. $114 \times 5 =$

GENERAL REVIEW 12

Solve each problem mentally.

1. 8 × 11 =

2. 7 × 6 =

3. 4,809 – 996 =

4. 2,019 + 489 =

5. Can 730 be divided by 10?

6. 1,364 + 123 =

7. 42 × 8 =

8. 168 ÷ 6 =

9. 2,411 – 12 =

10. 6 × 12 =

WEEK 50

GENERAL REVIEW 13

Solve each problem mentally.

1. 4,000 + 3,000 =

2. 2,716 + 999 =

3. 6,488 – 44 =

4. 49 × 8 =

5. Can 388 be divided by 2?

6. 567 ÷ 9 =

7. 219 + 403 + 117 + 211 =

8. 8 × 7 =

9. 5,689 + 9 =

10. 3,010 – 784 =

GENERAL REVIEW 14

Solve each problem mentally.

1. Can 528 be divided by 4?

2. 5,627 + 996 =

3. 12 × 12 =

4. 255 ÷ 3 =

5. Can 813 be divided by 3?

6. 3,314 + 15 =

7. 199 × 9 =

8. 2,403 + 482 =

9. 4,321 + 995 =

10. Can 390 be divided by 5?

GENERAL REVIEW 15

Solve each problem mentally.

1. 321 + 512 + 208 + 119 =

2. 8 × 9 =

3. 225 ÷ 9 =

4. 2,816 + 713 =

5. 1,257 + 7 =

6. 4,315 − 16 =

7. Can 632 be divided by 4?

8. 47 × 8 =

9. 8,356 − 187 =

10. 53 × 9 =

ANSWER KEY *Mental Math Level 3*

WEEK 1
1. 2,389
2. 4,495
3. 6,697
4. 8,875
5. 4,977
6. 5,798
7. 9,375
8. 7,668
9. 1,978
10. 4,978

WEEK 2
1. 9,716
2. 6,024
3. 3,268
4. 1,748
5. 8,922
6. 4,810
7. 7,750
8. 5,026
9. 9,946
10. 1,824

WEEK 3
1. 8,223
2. 1,435
3. 6,229
4. 5,241
5. 2,017
6. 3,747
7. 7,641
8. 4,331
9. 1,913
10. 9,927

WEEK 4
1. 3,844
2. 8,330
3. 4,257
4. 5,852
5. 2,471
6. 9,220
7. 6,346
8. 7,209
9. 2,110
10. 4,691

WEEK 5
1. 6,213
2. 4,921
3. 8,240
4. 2,661
5. 3,584
6. 5,295
7. 4,042
8. 7,515
9. 9,122
10. 5,292

WEEK 6
1. 5,839
2. 2,323
3. 7,274
4. 2,589
5. 4,280
6. 9,254
7. 5,315
8. 2,788
9. 8,121
10. 7,144

WEEK 7
1. 4,517
2. 6,623
3. 1,812
4. 3,711
5. 3,501
6. 8,712
7. 5,718
8. 8,240
9. 9,540
10. 5,054

WEEK 8
1. 7,000
2. 9,000
3. 7,000
4. 6,000
5. 9,000
6. 5,000
7. 9,000
8. 7,000
9. 8,000
10. 8,000

WEEK 9
1. 620
2. 750
3. 670
4. 1,150
5. 970
6. 1,300
7. 1,500
8. 1,230
9. 1,690
10. 1,930

WEEK 10
1. 9,226
2. 1,726
3. 5,238
4. 8,218
5. 4,217
6. 6,706
7. 7,435
8. 3,908
9. 2,833
10. 6,008

WEEK 11
1. 5,312
2. 8,415
3. 6,318
4. 7,030
5. 1,244
6. 4,732
7. 2,828
8. 9,344
9. 7,219
10. 6,937

WEEK 12
1. 8,000
2. 5,617
3. 1,170
4. 6,437
5. 1,925
6. 7,611
7. 7,833
8. 7,000
9. 2,113
10. 1,080

WEEK 13
1. 2,399
2. 5,599
3. 9,299
4. 3,599
5. 4,899
6. 6,299
7. 8,399
8. 1,899
9. 7,299
10. 9,799

WEEK 14
1. 2,028
2. 6,184
3. 629
4. 8,136
5. 4,169
6. 1,498
7. 5,321
8. 3,564
9. 7,029
10. 4,635

WEEK 15
1. 6,536
2. 8,124
3. 2,479
4. 4,793
5. 7,167
6. 281
7. 5,162
8. 3,354
9. 1,442
10. 4,376

WEEK 16
1. 1,439
2. 5,659
3. 8,189
4. 1,887
5. 7,240
6. 2,979
7. 7,695
8. 5,529
9. 4,258
10. 5,979

Week 17
1. 3,000
2. 7,000
3. 1,000
4. 4,000
5. 6,000
6. 2,000
7. 2,000
8. 5,000
9. 4,000
10. 2,000

Week 18
1. 4,299
2. 1,000
3. 7,346
4. 7,033
5. 4,638
6. 1,899
7. 3,329
8. 3,000
9. 3,264
10. 5,716

Week 19
1. 60
2. 36
3. 54
4. 24
5. 66
6. 48
7. 12
8. 42
9. 72
10. 18

Week 20
1. 28
2. 63
3. 21
4. 84
5. 49
6. 42
7. 35
8. 77
9. 14
10. 70

Week 21
1. 24
2. 56
3. 88
4. 48
5. 16
6. 64
7. 80
8. 32
9. 72
10. 96

Week 22
1. 90
2. 45
3. 27
4. 9
5. 63
6. 36
7. 18
8. 54
9. 72
10. 81

Week 23
1. 99
2. 132
3. 11
4. 55
5. 88
6. 121
7. 44
8. 33
9. 77
10. 22

Week 24
1. 45
2. 42
3. 72
4. 28
5. 132
6. 32
7. 63
8. 30
9. 84
10. 66

Week 25
1. 60
2. 120
3. 24
4. 84
5. 108
6. 144
7. 36
8. 72
9. 48
10. 132

Week 26
1. 616
2. 495
3. 333
4. 90
5. 696
6. 553
7. 156
8. 232
9. 201
10. 152

Week 27
1. 1,196
2. 2,994
3. 5,592
4. 1,995
5. 1,393
6. 3,591
7. 3,196
8. 2,697
9. 1,998
10. 5,391

Week 28
1. 688
2. 141
3. 234
4. 265
5. 444
6. 128
7. 665
8. 344
9. 384
10. 504

Week 29
1. 3,234
2. 3,628
3. 426
4. 2,457
5. 3,717
6. 2,696
7. 3,140
8. 2,334
9. 5,978
10. 1,920

Week 30
1. 801
2. 597
3. 544
4. 648
5. 216
6. 266
7. 465
8. 2,244
9. 1,797
10. 84

Week 31
1. Yes
2. No
3. No
4. Yes
5. Yes
6. Yes
7. No
8. Yes
9. Yes
10. No

Week 32
1. No
2. Yes
3. Yes
4. Yes
5. No
6. No
7. Yes
8. Yes
9. Yes
10. No

	WEEK **33**		WEEK **34**		WEEK **35**		WEEK **36**
1.	No	**1.**	Yes	**1.**	Yes	**1.**	Yes
2.	Yes	**2.**	No	**2.**	No	**2.**	No
3.	No	**3.**	Yes	**3.**	Yes	**3.**	No
4.	No	**4.**	No	**4.**	No	**4.**	No
5.	Yes	**5.**	Yes	**5.**	No	**5.**	Yes
6.	Yes	**6.**	Yes	**6.**	Yes	**6.**	No
7.	No	**7.**	No	**7.**	Yes	**7.**	No
8.	Yes	**8.**	No	**8.**	Yes	**8.**	Yes
9.	Yes	**9.**	Yes	**9.**	No	**9.**	No
10.	No	**10.**	Yes	**10.**	Yes	**10.**	Yes

	WEEK **37**		WEEK **38**		WEEK **39**		WEEK **40**
1.	Yes	**1.**	Yes	**1.**	No	**1.**	Yes
2.	Yes	**2.**	No	**2.**	Yes	**2.**	No
3.	No	**3.**	Yes	**3.**	Yes	**3.**	Yes
4.	No	**4.**	Yes	**4.**	No	**4.**	No
5.	No	**5.**	No	**5.**	No	**5.**	Yes
6.	Yes	**6.**	No	**6.**	Yes	**6.**	No
7.	No	**7.**	Yes	**7.**	No	**7.**	Yes
8.	No	**8.**	No	**8.**	Yes	**8.**	Yes
9.	Yes	**9.**	Yes	**9.**	No	**9.**	Yes
10.	No	**10.**	No	**10.**	Yes	**10.**	Yes

	WEEK **41**		WEEK **42**		WEEK **43**		WEEK **44**
1.	No	**1.**	No	**1.**	92	**1.**	65
2.	Yes	**2.**	Yes	**2.**	36	**2.**	23
3.	Yes	**3.**	Yes	**3.**	63	**3.**	52
4.	No	**4.**	Yes	**4.**	21	**4.**	82
5.	Yes	**5.**	Yes	**5.**	76	**5.**	63
6.	No	**6.**	Yes	**6.**	42	**6.**	72
7.	No	**7.**	No	**7.**	63	**7.**	47
8.	Yes	**8.**	Yes	**8.**	94	**8.**	29
9.	Yes	**9.**	Yes	**9.**	85	**9.**	43
10.	No	**10.**	Yes	**10.**	55	**10.**	74

	WEEK **45**		WEEK **46**		WEEK **47**		WEEK **48**
1.	2,358	**1.**	6	**1.**	7,025	**1.**	99
2.	1,108	**2.**	3,848	**2.**	865	**2.**	336
3.	99	**3.**	1,665	**3.**	4,792	**3.**	3,580
4.	7	**4.**	42	**4.**	5,962	**4.**	7,305
5.	132	**5.**	16	**5.**	Yes	**5.**	5,035
6.	9,000	**6.**	Yes	**6.**	32	**6.**	81
7.	No	**7.**	1,596	**7.**	7,028	**7.**	1,360
8.	42	**8.**	8	**8.**	3,199	**8.**	8
9.	1,594	**9.**	4,281	**9.**	60	**9.**	No
10.	590	**10.**	9,000	**10.**	No	**10.**	570

WEEK 49

1. 88
2. 42
3. 3,813
4. 2,508
5. Yes
6. 1,487
7. 336
8. 28
9. 2,399
10. 72

WEEK 50

1. 7,000
2. 3,715
3. 6,444
4. 392
5. Yes
6. 63
7. 950
8. 56
9. 5,698
10. 2,226

WEEK 51

1. Yes
2. 6,623
3. 144
4. 85
5. Yes
6. 3,329
7. 1,791
8. 2,885
9. 5,316
10. Yes

WEEK 52

1. 1,160
2. 72
3. 25
4. 3,529
5. 1,264
6. 4,299
7. Yes
8. 376
9. 8,169
10. 477